DOODLEBUGGING

DOODLEBUGGING

THE TREASURE HUNT FOR OIL

BY ELAINE SCOTT

FREDERICK WARNE NEW YORK LONDON

The author wishes to express her deepest appreciation to Carl H. Savit, doodlebugger of rare genius and senior vice-president, technology, of Western Geophysical Company of America, who generously took time to share a portion of his wit and wisdom with her.

And to Rhonda Boone, also from Western Geophysical, who graciously opened the company's photo files and aided in the selection of the photographs, thereby enabling all the children who read this book to go on the treasure hunt vicariously.

Frederick Warne & Co., Inc.
New York, New York

Printed in the U.S.A. by The Murray Printing Company
Book Design by Lucy Martin Bitzer

1 2 3 4 5 86 85 84 83 82

Library of Congress Cataloging in Publication Data

Scott, Elaine.
  Doodlebugging, the treasure hunt for oil.

  Includes index.
  Summary: Discusses the different methods used by geophysicists to locate petroleum.
    1. Petroleum—Juvenile literature.   2. Prospecting—Juvenile literature. [1. Petroleum. 2. Prospecting]
  I. Title.
  TN271.P4S36   622'.18282   82-4743
  ISBN 0-7232-6214-4   AACR2

Except where indicated, all photographs that appear in this book are the property of Western Geophysical Company of America, 10,001 Richmond Avenue, Houston, Texas, 77001, and were taken by Mike Fluitt. The author and publisher are grateful for their contribution.

This is for Parker, who inspired the book—and me.

CHAPTER 1

I'll bet lots of you who are reading this book have watched reruns of "The Beverly Hillbillies," a popular television series of the 1960s. In the beginning of each show, Jed Clampitt goes into the backyard to shoot a rabbit or a squirrel for dinner. When he shoots, he misses the game, but oil comes bubbling up from the ground, and—instantly—the Clampitts become rich and move to Beverly Hills.

If it were that easy to find oil today, lots of people would be rich. Unfortunately, oil has a way of hiding from us, and it takes more than a shell from a shotgun to scare it from its hiding place.

Oil wasn't always as difficult to find as it is now. Long ago, it used to lie in puddles on top of the ground. It had been squeezed up from inside the earth in much the same way you can squeeze soapsuds to the top of a soapy washcloth.

The North American Indians knew about these oil puddles. In fact, they used the oil they found in them for medicine, probably rubbing the sticky ooze on cuts, or perhaps even swallowing it.

Human beings have used oil in one form or another for centuries. In ancient Babylonia, around the time of King Nebuchadnezzar, the Babylonians were busy paving their streets with asphalt. Asphalt is a sticky, tarlike substance made up of oil, sand, and rock particles. Come to think about it, how many asphalt streets can you think of in your neighborhood? Asphalt has been around for a long time. It paves many of the streets and parks and playgrounds of America, just as it did in ancient Babylonia.

Today, much of the world's asphalt is produced from one enormous asphalt pit. It is called Pitch Lake, and it's located

—————————Pitch Lake, in Trinidad, is a lake of natural asphalt that continuously refills itself. Here some workers earlier in this century dig up some of the asphalt.

on the island of Trinidad in the Caribbean. The amazing thing about Pitch Lake is that it never runs out of asphalt. Whatever asphalt is taken from the lake today, nature will replace by tomorrow night. But that is asphalt. Mother nature does not replace our supplies of natural oil nearly that quickly.

To understand why it takes so long to replace the oil that we are taking from deep inside the earth today, it will help if you understand a little about how that oil was formed in the first place.

Scientists think that the story of oil began at least 250 million years ago. Ancient seas covered many parts of the earth that are dry land today. Fish and other marine animals lived in these seas, just as fish and animals do today. And, just as they do today, these ancient creatures ate the plant life that grew in the seas and around their shorelines.

While dinosaurs watched from the land, the seas rolled in and lapped at the shorelines. As the waves licked the land, they collected bits of earth and sand to carry back out to sea with them. More earth and sand were brought to the sea by rivers. These pieces of earth and sand drifted down through the ancient oceans and formed layers of mud and sand—the first step in the process of forming oil.

As the fish and plants that lived in these seas died, their bodies decayed. The decomposing bodies, which gave off fat and oily substances, slowly drifted down through the depths of the oceans, and the oily fats from them settled into the layers of sand and mud. This process repeated itself over and over again. The oceans continued to lay down more layers of mud and sand, and animals and plants continued to live, die, and decompose, sending more fats and oily substances into the new layers that formed.

As each new layer of sand and mud was laid down, it put pressure on the layers beneath it. Scientists estimate that these layers eventually exerted hundreds of tons of pressure on every square foot. That pressure began step two in the process of making oil.

You can see a single grain of sand on your hand. But if you were to smear mud or clay on your hand, it would be very difficult for you to see single grains of it. That's because the particles, or grains of matter, that make up mud and clay are much, much smaller than the grains of matter that make up sand.

When water is squeezed out of mud, it forms a layer of earth called *shale*. Because the particles of matter in shale are so small, the shale is very dense. Water cannot get through it. Neither can oil. Shale is, in a sense, waterproof.

When the grains of sand are squeezed together, they harden into a layer of earth called *sandstone*. Sandstone, because it is made of larger grains of matter, has holes in it, a little like a sponge.

Eventually, the tremendous pressure from each new layer of mud and sand hardened the older layers into shale and sandstone. At the very bottom of all these layers of shale and sandstone, there is a foundation layer of even older rocks.

While the pressure was squeezing the water out of the mud layers, changing them into shale and sandstone, it was also affecting the fats and oily substances that were in those layers. slowly changing them into crude oil. Some of the oil was squeezed to the top of the earth's surface by this pressure, and that oil formed the oil puddles already mentioned. Some of the oil did not squeeze to the surface but stayed in the mud and hardened with the mud into shale. We call shale layers that have oil hardened into them *oil shale*. Scientists have discovered that they can remove the oil from the shale by crushing the shale and heating it to about 900 degrees. The oil that is released from the shale by this process is called *shale oil*. The oil that didn't rise to the earth's surface or harden with the mud into shale settled into the holes in the sandstone, where it eventually became trapped. It is this oil that the world needs today.

If that were all there is to the formation of oil, you could drill anywhere on the surface of the earth and pump up oil from the holes in the sandstone below. And if that were the case, all of the countries of the world would have oil buried in the sandstone beneath them. We know that is not true. Some countries have plenty of oil and do not have to buy any from their neighbors. Other countries, like the United States, have a lot of oil but not enough to supply all their needs. They have to buy oil from countries that have more than they can use. Still other countries have no oil at all. They must buy every drop of it from another land.

The world's oil is not evenly distributed because the earth has never stayed still. The earth was not still 200 million years ago, and it hasn't stopped moving today. You know that the earth moves through space, but that is not the kind of movement we are talking about now. We are talking about the movement of the earth's crust—the very ground you stand on! If you think that it certainly doesn't feel like it's moving, you're right. Scientists think that North and South America are pulling away from Europe and Africa at a rate of about three centimeters a year—hardly a breathtaking pace! Nevertheless, they have been doing this for the last 200 million years or so; in that time, the Atlantic Ocean has widened from a

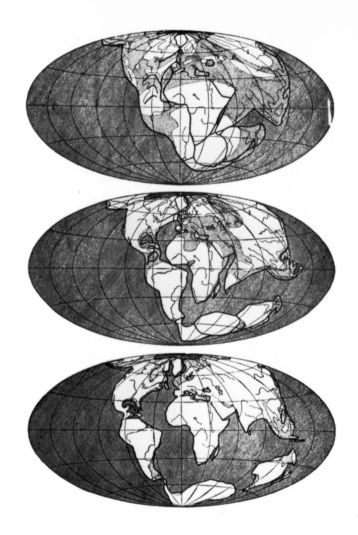

————————————These three maps illustrate the theory that long ago, during the time that oil was being formed, the continents fit together like pieces of a puzzle and that over millions of years they have drifted apart.

6

little crack in the land to the mighty body of water it is today.

If you look carefully at a world globe, you can see how the western coast of Africa could have, at one time, fit into the eastern coast of South America like parts of a giant jigsaw puzzle. Of course, it would not be a perfect fit today, because the oceans continue to wash the shorelines, and bit by bit, the shorelines of the world continue to change.

Not only has the crust of the earth been moving for millions of years, the rocks underneath the earth have heated and cooled many times, too. The heating and cooling of our planet caused the earth's surface to buckle. The buckling threw up entire mountain ranges on land that was once as flat as a tabletop. Those same movements caused entire oceans to disappear, leaving only the sand behind, and so a desert was born where fish once swam.

Of course, this is a simple explanation of a long and complicated process, but it is true that scientists have found elephant's teeth on the oceans' floors and the fossils of saltwater fish in the mountains of Wyoming. The earth's face did not always look the way it does today.

Deep inside the earth, as the continents buckled, stretched, and shifted, the layers of rocks, shale, and sandstone buckled, stretched, and shifted, too. Sometimes in the midst of all this change, a layer of dense shale would completely surround a layer of sandstone, creating an *oil trap*. This makes it impossible for any oil in the sandstone to float up and away. (Remember, oil is lighter than water, so it floats on top.) The oil that couldn't get away was trapped in an underground pool.

In order to picture these underground oil pools, it might help to remember the times you have squeezed water out of a soaked sponge and watched it run down your arm and into the sink or

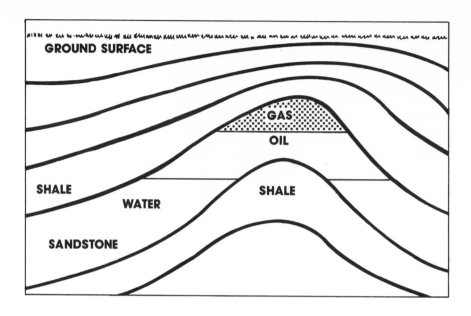

GAS

OIL

SHALE

SHALE

WATER

SANDSTONE

————————Far below the earth's crust, layers of shale surround layers of sandstone, forming a trap for the oil that floats on top of underground pools.

tub. As you squeezed the sponge, nothing stopped the water from escaping. Now, if you plopped a cereal bowl upside down on top of the sponge and some force squeezed the sponge while it was inside the bowl, the water in the sponge would still be forced out, but it would have nowhere to go. It would be trapped on top of the sponge, because of the bowl. And if you had soaked the sponge in oil and water, the oil would float on top of the water.

In nature, oil is trapped in the same way. Shale surrounds sandstone, as the cereal bowl surrounds the sponge. The moving and shifting of the earth forces the water and oil out of the holes in the sandstone, but it's trapped by the shale in an underground pool.

There are many kinds of oil traps inside the earth. Many of them are formed when dense shale surrounds porous sandstone. Some are formed when limestone surrounds a coral reef, and others are formed when solid rock covers broken-up rock. Some of the traps are shaped like a wedge, some like a doughnut, and some like an upside-down bowl. All of the traps were formed by changes in the earth over millions of years. The pulling and stretching of the continents caused some countries to have more traps with oil underneath their soil than other countries. Most of the traps beneath the earth's surface do not contain oil, but all of the oil that has been worth finding has been found in some type of natural trap.

In the past, no one thought oil was particularly important. American Indians taught the pioneers to use the oil from the oil puddles as medicine. And sometimes the pioneers turned the oil puddles into small businesses. Kit Carson sold oil from a puddle he owned to the settlers heading west, so they could grease their wagon wheels with it. But in those days—not much more than one hundred years ago—no one even dreamed of drilling for oil. There simply wasn't a demand for it.

Then, in the middle of the nineteenth century, something happened that changed people's minds about the value of oil. That something was the Industrial Revolution. When people hear the word "revolution," they usually think of war. This was a peaceful revolution, but like a war, it did change the way people lived.

During the Industrial Revolution, machines began doing the work that people had done by hand before. Factories sprang up, and many people left their farms and went to work in them, running the machines. The factories were dark and needed something to light them. Candles didn't work very well, and electric lights had not yet been invented.

There is an old expression, "Necessity is the mother of invention." It means that something is usually invented when people have a need for it. A Pennsylvania businessman named George Bissell began to wonder if the oil that was puddling up on his farm could be used for somthing besides grease and medicine. He decided to send a sample of his oil to Professor Benjamin Silliman at Yale University. Professor Silliman, who was a brilliant chemist, analyzed Bissell's sample and gave him a report that some people say actually began the oil industry.

————————————A symbol as well as a result of the Industrial Revolution, this oil refinery in Philadelphia during the 1920's struggled to meet the demands of the oil age.

Silliman reported that kerosene could be produced from oil, and kerosene would indeed light the lamps in the factories that were springing up across America. In addition to kerosene, Silliman reported that wax, or paraffin, for candles could be made from oil. Crude oil was refined to make lubricating oils for the factories' machines. Silliman discovered that kerosene could be refined to produce gasoline. Gasoline, however, exploded when people tried to burn it in kerosene lamps, so few people wanted gasoline.

Kerosene was the product that convinced Bissell, and others, that there was money to be made in the oil business. But in order to produce enough oil to make plenty of kerosene, Bissell had to come up with a way to bring it out of the earth without digging a pit for it or gathering it by hand from the puddles.

At the time, another man from Pennsylvania, Samuel Kier, had drilled for salt on his farm and—much to his dismay—had struck oil instead. Many salt miners were having this kind of problem, and when they struck oil, they closed their salt mines down in disgust. Kier decided to do something with his oil. He bottled it and sold it as medicine, calling it Rock Oil.

Bissell had seen a bottle of Kier's medicine, which had a picture of a derrick on it because salt miners used derricks to drill for salt water, or brine. Bissell looked at Kier's medicine and thought, Why not drill for oil the way you drill for salt water?

Bissell and his partner, Jonathan Eveleth, formed an oil company, and in 1857, the two partners hired a man named Edwin L. Drake to drill what they hoped would be an oil well on Bissell's farm in Titusville, Pennsylvania. Drake was really a retired railroad conductor, but Bissell gave him the title of Colonel because he thought that would impress the people around Titusville. The title stuck, and to this day, Edwin Drake is known in the oil business as Colonel Drake.

Like the salt miners, Drake decided to go after the oil on Bissell's property by first digging a pit. But Drake's pit kept filling up with water. So instead of beginning with a pit, then erecting a derrick, as the salt miners did, Drake decided to drill from the very start. Like many good ideas, Drake's sounded fine until he tried it out. He soon discovered that the soft earth was caving in around the stem of the drill he was using. In order to stop this from happening, Drake came up with one of the best ideas of all. He decided to support the soft sides of the hole he was drilling by putting his drill inside something strong and firm. Drake lined his hole with an iron pipe. This pipe was called a *casing*, and casings are still used today when people drill for oil.

Drake dropped his casing into the well and then drilled away, all the way down to sixty-nine feet. That was an awfully deep hole, and nothing was happening. Then, on August 27, 1859, something black and sticky and smelly began to seep into the bottom of that deep hole. Slowly the treasure filled the hole, until it came very close to the top. Drake had struck oil in Pennsylvania, and the petroleum age began.

News of Drake's well spread, and soon people began drilling for oil all around the United States. In the 1880s Kentucky, Ohio, Illinois, and Indiana joined Pennsylvania as oil-producing states. Kansas got into the act in 1894. (Texas was a latecomer, starting only in 1901.)

Until 1900, all these wells in all these states concentrated on producing one thing from the crude oil they pumped up from deep inside the earth: kerosene. Kerosene to light the factories' lamps—that was the product everyone wanted. The refineries produced gasoline, too, as a result of refining the kerosene, but no one wanted gasoline, so it was frequently dumped in creeks and rivers to get rid of it. In the late 1800s there seemed to be little use for gasoline.

But by the beginning of the twentieth century, the need for gasoline was becoming more apparent. In 1900 gas lights—and even some electric lights—were replacing the kerosene lamps that had been so popular. And a strange new method of transportation—the horseless carriage—appeared in America. In 1900, there were about 8,000 of these creatures in the United States. Then a man named Henry Ford had an idea about mass production, and by 1910, there were over 450,000 automobiles in America. Horseless carriages fed on gasoline instead of oats. And they all had big appetites.

As America and the rest of the world moved into the twentieth century, automobiles were not the only products that demanded oil. Oil is burned to generate electricity, and soon electricity was needed for many more things than lighting a lamp. Refrigerators replaced iceboxes for cooling, and electric heaters replaced wood-burning fireplaces for warmth. Asphalt, which can be made from petroleum, paved many of the streets that were soon carrying trucks and buses, as well as cars, from here to there. Trains and planes, all of them using petroleum products, crisscrossed the nation. Paraffin and polyester, petroleum jelly and paint—all of these products and hundreds more come from oil. Oil rapidly became a very valuable commodity, and many people looked for places to drill for the black gold, as it quickly came to be called.

The beginning of the petroleum age saw a new breed of treasure hunter, the *wildcatter*. A wildcatter is a person who drills for oil in a certain spot just because he thinks it might

—————————————The development of the gasoline-powered auto-
mobile made oil a more valuable treasure to hunt, especially when
mass production made automobiles available to hundreds of thousands.

be there. After Drake's well came in, wildcatters chose to drill
their oil wells in similar spots, places that already had oil puddles on the ground. Some of the wildcatters noticed that oil
seemed to be found if they drilled into the top of a gentle hill,
or bulge, on the earth's surface. These early wildcatters knew
nothing about oil traps, but that is exactly what they were
drilling into when they drilled into those hills. Sometimes they
were lucky and hit oil, and sometimes they were unlucky, for
many of the traps were empty.

The demand for oil continued to increase, and soon all of
the easy-to-find oil had been found. Oil companies were drilling

more and finding less, and the drilling was *very* expensive. Someone had to figure out a better way to find oil than just guessing where it might be. And so rather quickly, the oil companies looked to *geology* for help.

Geology is the study of the earth—its crust and the layers of rock and shale and sandstone that lie beneath the crust. In the early days of the oil industry, geologists were often called "mud smellers" and "pebble pickers" because of their interest in the dirt and rocks that make up our planet. By studying the earth, geologists came up with the theory that it had stretched and changed over the centuries and that oil was held in traps beneath its surface. The geologists wondered if their theory about the movement of the earth was correct, so they looked to another kind of scientist to help them find the answer. That scientist was the *physicist*. To put it very simply, a physicist is a scientist who studies the way things are moved. A physicist understands a lot about gravity and force—things falling down and things pushing against one another. When the geologist and the physicist began to work together to understand how things move inside the earth, a new breed of scientist resulted. That scientist was called a *geophysicist*.

The geophysicist is a modern-day treasure hunter. Understanding how the earth was made and how it moves, the geophysicist uses sophisticated scientific methods to look for oil that has stayed hidden inside the earth for ages. The geophysicist's search takes him on a hunt that is every bit as exciting and adventurous—and even dangerous—as any hunt for hidden treasure has ever been.

Wildcatter, mud slinger, pebble picker—the oil industry has many nicknames for the people who work in it. A geophysicist has a nickname, too. He's called a *doodlebugger*. Not all geophysicists are doodlebuggers, however. That nickname belongs to the geophysicists who actually travel around the world hunting for oil.

In the beginning, "doodlebugger" was a teasing kind of name. No one is certain how it started, but some people think it came about because the earliest doodlebuggers used water witches, or divining rods, to hunt for oil, and a nickname for a water witch is "doodlebug."

A water witch is a forked stick, shaped a little like a Y. When a family wanted to locate a good spot on their property to drill a water well, they would hire someone to come and "witch" the ground. The water witcher would cut a fresh (it had to be fresh!) Y-shaped branch from a tree and, holding it by its two "handles," walk along the ground until the stem of the witch pointed down. It was there that the family drilled for water.

As oil became more and more difficult to locate by wildcatting, some people tried witching for it. When the wildcatters saw the first geophysicists trying out water witches, they laughed at them and called them "doodlebuggers." The water witch is not a very reliable instrument for locating water—or oil, for that matter—and it was soon replaced by increasingly complicated scientific instruments. People still call today's geophysicists "doodlebuggers," but no one's laughing any more.

Doodlebuggers use three major instruments to look for oil: the *magnetometer*, the *gravimeter*, and the *seismograph*. This book will be about doodlebuggers who use the seismograph, but you should know a little bit about the other instruments.

A magnetometer is a tiny instrument shaped like a little bomb. It is often trailed from an airplane, attached to the plane by a cable. All rocks are magnetic, to some degree, and the magnetometer is used to measure the earth's magnetic field to see if the area being measured is worth the time and trouble to send a doodlebugging crew in with a seismograph. Using a magnetometer, the doodlebuggers can tell how thick the layers of shale, sandstone, or limestone are. If the layers are thin, oil is probably not trapped within them, and the doodlebuggers will not bother to explore the area. However, if those layers, which are called *sedimentary rock*, are nice and thick, doodlebuggers assume oil could be trapped there, so they may decide to look at the area more carefully with the seismograph. A magnetometer is not always trailed from an airplane, but it can cover a lot of area quickly if it is.

The gravimeter is an instrument that looks like a small box. A doodlebugger places the gravimeter on the ground in the spot that he wants to explore. The gravimeter measures the force of gravity at that spot. Gravity is the force that pulls objects to the center of the earth. Heavy, dense rocks have more weight (and so, more gravitational force) than do the lighter, oil-bearing rocks. So you can see that a gravimeter can be very helpful in finding those lighter rock layers.

The doodlebuggers in this book rely on the seismograph to help them locate the places where oil might be found. The seismograph is an instrument that is able to measure the intensity of the earth's movements. A seismograph measures the earth's violent movements, like earthquakes, and it also measures that incredibly slow shifting and stretching that goes

A seemingly magic box that listens and records, the seismograph is the most important instrument the doodlebuggers use.

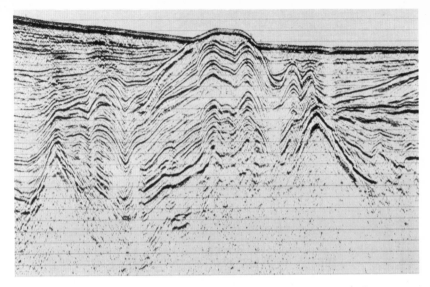

———————————————Seismic records from the seismograph are processed later by giant computers. The result is called a seismic section (see chapter 10). This seismic section clearly shows the bulges in the underground layers of shale and sandstone. Could oil be trapped below?

on all the time without our feeling it. The seismograph can also measure the length of time it takes a vibration to travel from deep inside the earth to its surface. The measurements of intensity and time that the seismograph makes are recorded on a piece of magnetic tape called a *seismogram*, or *seismic record*. By reading seismic records, a geophysicist can tell how strong a particular earthquake was and exactly where, beneath the surface of the earth, the trembling began.

But seismographs have other uses besides measuring the strength of earthquakes. Sometimes they are used to help choose the site to build a nuclear power plant. It is extremely important that a nuclear power plant be built on land that is stable—that is, land that is not likely to move because of a *fault*. A fault is any break in the layers of rock beneath the earth. Earthquakes occur more frequently in areas where there are faults. An earthquake could cause tremendous damage to a nuclear power plant and as a result, the area around the plant could be contaminated with radioactive products. Records from a seismograph show whether the land in question is safe to build on, and occasionally doodlebuggers are asked to make this kind of record with their seismographs.

But a doodlebugger's main job is not to measure earthquakes or check on the safety of land. Instead, doodlebuggers *cause* earthquakes and then measure what they have done with their seismographs. The seismic record from the seismograph becomes a kind of treasure map that gives the doodlebugger clues to where oil and gas might be hidden.

An earthquake can be a terrible thing. The earth heaves and trembles violently. Sometimes huge cracks appear in its crust. Entire cities can be destroyed. But there are other kinds of earthquakes, too. Doodlebuggers cause them to happen, and instead of being destructive, these earthquakes give doodlebuggers important information about finding oil.

The doodlebugger can control the violence of his earthquake. Actually, all he does is give the earth a little shake—the surface moves up and down less than the thickness of a human hair. But that shake he gives the earth must go at least 20,000 or 30,000 feet deep.

A doodlebugger shakes the earth three different ways: with explosive charges, packed into a hole he has drilled; with a huge vibrating machine that gives the earth tremendous shakes; or with powerful blasts of air from an air gun that go deep into the ocean floor. No matter how the doodlebugger causes an earthquake, this method of looking for oil is called *seismic reflection*, and it is the most popular method of all.

It takes more than one doodlebugger to make an earthquake —it takes an entire crew of them. If doodlebuggers shake the earth by dropping explosives into a hole, they are called a *shooting crew*. If they shake the earth with vibrators, they are called a *vibrator crew*. Doodlebuggers who work at sea, shaking the ocean with blasts of air from an air gun are called a *marine crew*. This book will allow you to visit all three types of doodlebugging crews as they search for oil all over the world. But before the visits begin, you should understand a little about how seismic reflection works.

Have you ever listened to a tuning fork? When you strike

the tuning fork it vibrates, and those vibrations make the sound that you hear. As the earth shakes, its vibrations also make a sound, but the sound is too faint or too low in pitch for the doodlebugger to hear. So he uses a microphone to hear it.

If a doodlebugger is working on land, he calls his microphones *geophones*. If a doodlebugger is working at sea, he calls them *hydrophones*—"geo" for land and "hydro" for water. Because everyone in the oil business seems to like nicknames, doodlebuggers call the geophones *jugs*. The people who place them on the ground are called *juggies*.

Geophones or hydrophones are attached to a seismograph by wires. The wires are protected by a thick, black cable that covers them. The microphones pick up the sounds inside the earth and convert those sounds to electrical signals. The signals then go through the wires and on to the seismograph. The seismograph records the sounds and spits out the seismic record. This record is very, very important. Like a treasure map, a seismic record tells the doodlebuggers if traps containing oil are hiding beneath the earth where the doodlebugger is shaking.

You may wonder how someone can tell where an oil trap is just by listening. It works a little like this. Have you ever watched someone knock on a wall to find the stud—the piece of wood frame—that is behind the plaster on the wall? Sometimes people do this when they want to drive a nail into the wall to hang a picture. They want to be certain that the nail goes into the wooden stud. The wall makes a certain sound when they knock, and as they come close to the stud behind the wall, the sound changes. Try it yourself. Knock on a wall and see if you can hear the sound change as you come to the stud. What you are actually hearing is an echo. The wall vi-

23

——————The geophones look like they are strung on cords of licorice, but these cables are definitely not edible!

brates when you knock on it, and the sound from that vibration echos back to you. Because the stud is close to the surface of the wall, the echo there does not have far to travel, so the sound is different than it is when there is no stud for it to bounce off of.

The doodlebugger's shakes from his vibrators, blasts from his air guns, and shots from explosives all send sound deep into the layers of the earth, just as your fist sent sound—or energy—deep into the wall. The doodlebugger's seismograph measures the time it takes for the sound to enter the earth, bounce off the layers of rock below, and return to the surface. The longer it takes for the sound to return, the deeper the layer of rock lies. Traps that could contain oil tend to make a bulge in their particular layer of rock, making that layer look a little like an underground hill. Doodlebuggers are looking for these hidden hills. If the doodlebugger shakes the earth on top of the hill, the sound will return to his seismograph more quickly than it will when he shakes the earth on either side of the hill. The sounds that the seismograph records tell the doodlebugger when he is over a trap, just as the sounds in your wall told you when you were over a stud.

The seismograph measures the time it takes for the sound

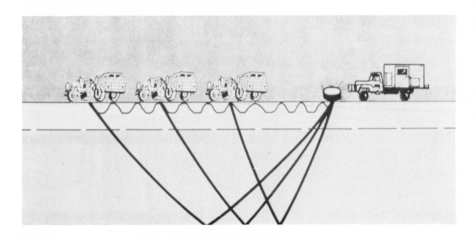

—————————The vibrators' shakes send energy into the earth, where it bounces off the rock layers below and back to the listening geophone.

to return to the surface, and how strong the sound is. Weaker sounds mean the doodlebugger is shaking over harder rock. Stronger sounds mean he is over softer—and possibly oil-bearing—rock.

When doodlebuggers send energy into the earth with an explosive charge, they say they are taking a *shot*. And the place where the explosive goes off is called the *shot point*. If the energy for the earthquakes comes from a vibrator, the doodlebuggers say they are *shaking*, and the spot where the mighty vibrators shake the earth is called the *vibrator point*. Doodlebuggers shoot or shake at many points along a path that has been decided upon before they begin. The path that the doodlebuggers follow is called the *line*. "Shooting a line" is doodlebugging talk for exploring a particular area for oil traps.

The client, usually an oil company, who hires the doodlebuggers to shoot the line decides where the line will be. Sometimes it is in nice, flat, dry pasture right here in America. Sometimes the line goes through dark, smelly, humid jungles in the Far East or South America. Sometimes the line runs across the North Sea, and sometimes it snakes over the shifting, hot sands of the Saudi Arabian desert or over the frozen tundra of the arctic. But no matter where it is—close to home, or very far away indeed—the doodlebugger is always ready to go. And this time, you'll go with him.

It's always easiest to look for something in a place that's close by and easy to reach, so we'll begin looking for oil right here in the United States. We'll watch a crew that is working in California, but we could just as easily be watching a crew at work in Texas or Louisiana. Texas, Louisiana, and California are our country's largest oil-producing states. Oklahoma, Wyoming, Alaska, Kansas, Missouri, Montana, and Illinois are the other top producers, but oil has been discovered in many other states, too. You may have noticed that Pennsylvania, where the petroleum industry got started, is not even on the list of top producers any more. But we still get oil from Pennsylvania, and we are looking for it in Tennessee and Florida and many other states, too.

Let's assume that an oil company has hired a geophysical exploration company (that's the proper name for a doodle-bugging company) to look for oil on land it has leased in California. It may surprise you to know that most oil companies do not own the land where they drill for oil—they merely have an *oil lease*. An oil lease means that the oil company is paying the landowner for the privilege of looking for oil on his property. If the oil company finds oil, it will pay the landowner a *royalty* on the oil that is pumped from the well. A royalty is a share of the earnings that something makes. For example, an author is paid a royalty on each copy of his book that is sold. In this case, the landowner is paid a royalty on each barrel of oil that is pumped from his land.

The United States is one of the few countries in the world that permits its citizens to own the *mineral rights* to the oil or other valuable deposits that might be under their property. In

Across mountains and valleys, through jungles and deserts, the doodlebuggers track down oil treasure. This doodlebugger is laying out her geophones across some rough terrain in western North America.

many other countries, the citizens own only the *surface rights* to their land. In other words, they only own the dirt, not the oil or gold or silver that might be buried beneath that dirt. The government of the country owns all the mineral rights and collects all the royalties for any oil or precious metal that is taken from the land.

Once an oil company has obtained an oil lease, it is time for the doodlebuggers to go into action. The first thing they must do is obtain permission to go on the property. Even though the oil company has leased it, the geophysical exploration company must get permission for their people, trucks, and heavy equipment to move onto the land. The person who obtains this permission is called a *permit agent.*

The permit agent explains to the landowner that the doodlebuggers will fill in the holes that their explosives have left if a shooting crew is going to be used. Sometimes a cow or other livestock wanders too close to the blasting area and gets blasted itself. The permit agent explains that his company will pay for the value of the cow if something like that should happen. In general, the permit agent tells the landowner that the doodlebuggers will be careful while they are on his property.

When the landowner understands that his property will be protected, he gives his permission for the crew to enter. Sometimes, however, he forgets to tell anyone else who works for him that it's all right for the doodlebuggers to be there.

Once, on a ranch in California, a group of doodlebuggers rolled onto the land with all their equipment, ready to get to work. They were greeted by the ranch foreman, who had a shotgun tucked under his arm. The landowner had forgotten to tell his foreman that the crew had permission to be on the land. A few quick phone calls cleared up the misunderstand-

———————————A landowner keeps a careful eye on the doodle-buggers as they make their way across his property.

ing, and the crew went to work, and no one had to pick buck-shot out of anyone else.

As soon as the crew is on the land, the crew's *surveyors* go to work. A surveyor is a person who can accurately measure the boundaries of a piece of land by using special instruments and mathematics. On a doodlebugging crew, it is the surveyor's job to measure the land to be certain the line—the path that will be shaken—is exactly where the oil company wants it.

Let's say the crew we are watching is a shooting crew. If they have never explored this area before, they will want to have a day or two of experimental shooting until they can decide on the proper amount of explosive to use to make the earth shake. On rocky land, where the explosives will be packed into shallow holes no deeper than six to eight feet, anywhere from three to eleven holes will be drilled at each shot point, and around a pound of explosive will be packed into each hole. Doodlebuggers call multihole shots a *pattern*. If they are working in land that is easy to drill, then only one shot hole will be drilled, but it will be a deep one—probably about sixty to eighty feet—and about ten pounds of explosive will be packed into the bottom of that one hole. The *shooter* on the crew is the doodlebugger who is responsible for all the explosives. He sees to it that they are stored carefully and used safely. Based on the experimental shooting, he decides how much explosive should be used for the shots. It is the shooter's job to arm the blaster that will set the shots.

The *driller* is the person who drives the drill trucks and mans the drills when they make the holes for the explosive charges.

The juggies lay out the geophones and cables. In order to be able to listen properly when the shot goes off, the geophones must be perfectly vertical to the ground. Vertical means

——————————Work starts early for a doodlebugging crew. Here the juggies unload the geophones and cables, getting ready to begin their day.

straight up and down, so as the juggies lay them out, they stand them at attention. The geophones and cables are heavy, and the juggies must carry them, sometimes walking along the line for miles and stooping at each survey stake to push the geophone spike into the ground.

The geophones and cables are attached to the seismograph. The seismograph and the other seismic instruments are installed in the back of a truck called the *recording truck*. The recording truck looks a little like a camper, but there is no space for beds and chairs. There is room only for the instruments and the person who is going to run them. This camperlike space that holds the instruments is called the *doghouse*. It has no room to spare, and any doodlebugger who enters the doghouse probably feels as if he has crawled into a real one!

The *observer* is the member of the crew who runs the instruments. Sometimes he has an assistant called a *junior observer*. The observer spends most of his time in the doghouse, observing the seismic instruments. He must be certain they are functioning properly, and he knows immediately when they are not. If the seismograph is not working properly, then the information it records will be incorrect. So all day long, closed up in his doghouse, the observer watches the seismograph and the piece of paper with the wiggly lines—the seismic record—that is slowly spit from it. Because the seismic record is the treasure map, leading—it is hoped—to the buried treasure of oil, the observer makes certain the map is accurate. From his seat in the doghouse the observer fires the shot, pushing a button that sets off the blaster, if he is on a shooting crew, or makes the vibrators shake, if he is on a vibrator crew.

Now we are ready to shoot. The geophones are in place. The explosive charge has been packed in the hole, and the shooter

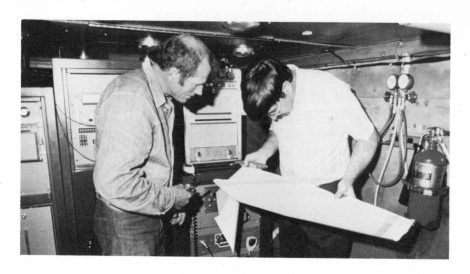

——————————————Snug in their doghouse, the observer and the junior observer keep a careful check on the seismic record as the seismograph slowly sends it out.

has armed the blaster, so it will fire when the observer pushes the button. A warning is sounded, and everyone moves away from the place where the shot will go off. People who are standing near a geophone do not move. The microphones are so sensitive that they pick up the sound of a footstep, and the only sound the geophones should hear are the echos that come back from the insides of the earth.

The shot goes off, and you can feel the earth rumble underneath your feet. In the doghouse, the seismic instruments come to life, and the wiggly lines begin to appear on the piece of paper. The hunt for black gold has begun!

When the shot goes off, and the instruments function properly, the crew is ready to move all its equipment down the line and do it again. The recording truck may stay where it is for

34

a while. It does not move with each shot, but the juggies move the geophones to the area of the next shot, and the shooter arms the blaster. In the recording truck, the observer triggers the shot; the instruments spring into action, and another seismic record is made. It goes on and on like this all day long. Slowly the crew inches over the land, shaking and listening, shaking and listening.

Since this shooting crew is working in California, you can assume that they are not too far from a town. So, at the end of the day's shooting, the crew returns to that town for some well-deserved rest. The town is the crew's headquarters for the time it takes them to shoot all the lines the client wants. A client usually wants more than one line shot in each leased area; the layout of the lines is called the *prospect.*

A man called a *party manager* has rented office space in the town. The office space may be a motel room or an empty warehouse or, if nothing else is available, perhaps the corner of a gas station. The office of a doodlebugging field crew is rarely very fancy.

The office is managed by the party manager, who supervises all the doodlebuggers on the crew. The party manager understands all the jobs of the doodlebugging crew, from juggie to observer. He is responsible for paying the men on his crew and making certain the operation runs smoothly. He keeps the client informed about the progress the crew is making, too. The party manager hires, and sometimes fires, most of the doodlebuggers on his crew.

When all of the lines on the prospect have been shot, the doodlebuggers are ready to move on to the next job. But first, they go back and repair any damage their equipment caused. The shot holes are filled in. Any ruts the trucks made in the pasture are smoothed out. If, happily, no cows wandered up on a shot, there won't be a need to replace them. The ranch will look as if no one had been there, and it will stay that way unless traps were found and the client thinks they might be full of oil. If that is the case, oil wells will spring up on the ranch where the doodlebuggers' trucks once were. But by then those trucks and drills, men and machines, will have moved on to the next job.

The client is the person who decides whether or not to use a shooting crew or a vibrator crew to work the line. Some geophysicists think that a vibrator gives the earth the kind of shake that produces the clearest sounds for the seismograph. Other geophysicists prefer to shake the ground with explosive charges. Many factors influence the choice of which type of crew to use, and sometimes the terrain—the type of land the line runs through—makes the decision for the client.

Shooting crews, for example, are a lot more practical in a swamp, and shaking crews work much better if the line runs through a town. If a line ran through the swamps of southern Louisiana, the client would probably want to use a shooting crew, because the drills are rather lightweight, especially when you compare them with the tremendous weight of a vibrator. Heavy vibrators would sink into the swamps, tearing them up so badly that they could not be restored. A shooting crew would be a good choice for the swamps, because it would not damage the environment there.

On the other hand, an oil company once wanted to shoot a line through downtown Los Angeles. Obviously it isn't practical to inch through a city drilling holes and setting off explosive charges in the earth. Vibrators can shake the earth without doing any surface damage that would have to be repaired later, so in this case the client chose to use a shaking crew. The vibrators shook their way right through the downtown section of Los Angeles, just as they shake their way through cities and towns all over the world. Perhaps you have seen these strange-looking caravans working their way through the main street of your town.

————————————The fir trees keep watch as the doodlebugging parade passes by on its way north.

There is one swampy area where vibrators are used, but it's a frozen swamp. Actually, it is the *tundra* of the arctic, near the North Pole. The tundra is a vast, treeless, marshy plain that freezes absolutely solid during the long arctic winters. The tundra can be easily scarred by men and their machines and equipment during the few summer months when it thaws out a bit, so the doodlebuggers work up there only during the long arctic winter. Let's follow a shaking crew to the North Slope of Alaska.

As winter settles in, the doodlebuggers prepare to head north from wherever they were working during the summer. The families move to Anchorage or Fairbanks, and the children settle into a new school once again. Doodlebuggers' children have to get used to being the new kids in class—it happens to them quite a bit.

When the families are settled, the men drive the giant vibrators up the Alaskan Highway, through the towns and cities, and far beyond civilization until, at last, they roll onto the tundra of the arctic. It is quite a parade. Perhaps there will be five vibrators, the recording truck, and trucks to carry the cables and geophones, food and office supplies.

Arctic winters are cold and dark. In the afternoon the temperature may warm up to forty degrees below zero. For about two months during the winter, the sun never shines, and it is dark all day long. Snow and ice cover the earth as far as you can see.

Unlike the shooting crew in California, who were able to return to town at the end of each day's work, these doodlebuggers will be staying up here on the tundra, away from their families for weeks at a time. There is no town nearby, so they bring along their own living quarters.

——————————At times in the Arctic, the sun doesn't shine at all. At other times it rises only as far as in this picture. In their trailer camp, the doodlebuggers must get used to this strange phenomenon.

Whisker-freezing weather in the Arctic doesn't stop this surveyor from mapping the doodlebugging line.

The doodlebuggers live in trailers when they are not working. There are several of these bright-red trailers in the doodlebuggers' camp. There are trailers for the men to sleep in, and trailers to eat in. There is a trailer that serves as an office for the party manager, and there is a trailer that is more or less like a living room. The men can go there to visit or read or just relax after a long day's work.

Surveyors and juggies, dressed in fur-lined parkas and arctic boots and gloves, map the line and place the geophones, working their way through snow that can sometimes come up to their waist. Once the jugs are in place, the crew is ready to begin a few days of experimental shakes, and now it is time for the giant vibrators to come into action.

40

A vibrator is a tremendous piece of machinery—most of them weigh more than thirteen tons. It is mounted on either a truck or a buggy. A vibrator mounted on a buggy has a joint in the middle that allows it to twist a bit, and they are used in areas, such as a jungle, where the line twists and snakes through the underbrush. Since the terrain on the North Slope is flat, the vibrators used up here are on trucks. The vibrators have a three-by-seven-foot baseplate made out of thick steel. The plate itself weighs 3,900 pounds and is attached to the vibrator underneath its middle.

When it is time for the shake to begin, the plates lower to the ground and there they begin to shake the earth. Sometimes

Rearing up like an angry animal, the vibrator gives the earth a good shake.

41

——————————Nearly two tons of steel make a powerful vibrator plate.

these huge plates shake the earth beginning at a rate of eight times a second and moving up, in a period of sixteen seconds, to the point where they are shaking the earth forty times a second. Sometimes they begin to shake it six times a second and move up to eighty times a second. Sometimes the doodle-buggers start the shake at the faster rate and move it down to the slower rate. The rate that the vibrator pad shakes the ground—eight up to forty a second, or six up to eighty a second —is called the *sweep*. Doodlebuggers decide on the sweep by considering the kind of geology that is below the earth where they are working and by doing several days of sweep comparison tests to see how much the earth should be shaken in order to get back the best echoes.

When the observer decides on the sweep that he wants, he enters that sweep into a computer on the recording truck. When the observer pushes the start button, all five vibrators will begin to shake precisely together, at the rate the observer wants.

Now it is time for the first shake. The vibrator operators have driven their huge machines into place on the line. Because the vibrator seismograph is made differently from the shooting crew's seismograph, it records only the sounds from the shake and is able to ignore the other kinds of sounds that might be around, such as moving trucks or people walking. A vibrator crew can go about its business while the earth is being shaken without worrying about spoiling the seismic record. When the observer is satisfied that everything is ready, he pushes the button that begins this man-made earthquake.

Slowly the steel pads descend from the vibrators' middles, and the operators, riding in the cabs above, are lifted into the air as the machines rear up like a small herd of bucking metal

43

——————————Inside the cab of the vibrator, the doodlebuggers go for a ride as the vibrator shakes the earth.

elephants. The observer has decided on a 8-40 sweep, so the earth begins to shake at eight times a second, and sixteen seconds later, it will be shaking forty times a second. The geophones listen to the sounds from the shake and send those sounds back to the seismograph which measures and records them on the seismic record. When the shake is over, the cabs of the vibrators lower and their giant wheels are on the ground once again. The baseplates retreat into the vibrators' middles, and the crew is ready to move down the line for the second shake. The process goes on all day, and the seismograph records the sounds of the trembling earth on a reel of magnetic tape. The reel of tape gets longer and longer as the day wears on.

At the end of the day, the doodlebuggers return to their trailers. The vibrator operators park their machines, but they do not cut the engines off. The engines run twenty-four hours a day because the bitter sub-zero temperatures of the arctic make the metal in the machines very brittle. When things become brittle, they can break easily. In order to avoid broken engine parts, the vibrators' engines are kept running so they can stay warm. If a vibrator operator shuts off his engine, chances are his vibrator would not start the next day.

Doodlebuggers all over the world take good care of their equipment, but things do break down, so mechanics are very important members of doodlebugging crews—especially crews that are working in remote areas like the North Slope. Sometimes mechanics travel from crew to crew, flying in by helicopter if necessary, to keep the machinery in good running condition.

This shaking crew on the North Slope cannot go to the local hamburger place for dinner, so supplies of food are brought in to the trailer camp periodically, and each day the cook prepares breakfast and dinner for forty or so hungry doodlebuggers. Lunch is frequently skipped; when the line is vibrated away from the camp, it takes too long for the doodlebuggers to leave the line and return to camp for lunch. Everyone is anxious to find oil, and the doodlebuggers hurry to complete each job as quickly as possible.

Sometimes the cook winds up fixing three meals a day, and he may have to fix them for several days on end. This happens when a *whiteout* closes down the shaking on the North Slope. During a whiteout, blowing snow or falling snow—or a combination of both—fills the air. A person cannot see his finger if he holds it at the end of his nose. The whole world becomes a swirling mass of white snow. The bright-red trailers quickly become invisible, and the doodlebuggers have to use guide ropes to get from the sleeping trailers to the dining trailers.

Frostbite is always a possible danger, so the doodlebuggers stay in their trailers as much as possible until the whiteout is over and they can return to vibrating the line. Sometimes a whiteout lasts only a few hours; often it lasts for days.

All through the long arctic winter, the doodlebuggers work. They get home to Fairbanks or Anchorage to see their families only once in a while. But when the spring thaw begins, their job on the tundra comes to an end. As the tundra softens, the doodlebuggers get ready to leave.

The trailers are moved out, and the vibrators are driven or shipped to their next location, depending on where it is. The men return to their families, and the families prepare to make another move. Perhaps they will move a few hundred miles; perhaps they will move across the world.

Doodlebugging companies try to keep their vibrators and drills, trucks and equipment, doodlebuggers and their families, in the same general area, but it isn't always possible to do this. However, some doodlebugging families have lived in one area so long that they have actually bought houses and settled down. The children have gone to the same school for years at a time. But that is not a typical situation. It happens only when the area has many traps, and the oil companies want many, many lines shot through many, many prospects. That kind of work can take years to complete. Most doodlebugging jobs do not last that long, and the doodlebugging equipment is too expensive to be allowed to sit idle while the doodlebuggers wait to be offered a job that is right around the corner from their last one. Occasionally a doodlebugging company uses the time between jobs to do some exploring on its own.

When a doodlebugging company is working for a client, the information that it gets from the seismic record belongs to the client, of course. It is secret information, and the doodlebuggers do not share it with anyone else. As in any good treasure hunt, no one wants the competition to get there before he does, so no one shares his treasure map.

However, if a doodlebugging company explores a prospect on its own, things work a little differently. The doodlebuggers usually shoot their lines on land that belongs to the government of the country they are in. The United States government offers oil leases on land that is not privately owned. Other governments, of course, own the mineral rights to all the land anyway.

The doodlebuggers obtain permission from the government to shoot lines on a prospect on *speculation*. Speculation means the doodlebuggers have no idea who will buy their information once they get it. After the doodlebuggers shoot or vibrate the lines and get good, clear records of what the earth below the prospect looks like, they will offer these records for sale. Sometimes they sell them to more than one oil company. Each oil company realizes that its competitors are buying the information, too, but it costs the company far less to buy this shared information than it would cost it to hire the doodlebuggers to work only for it. After they buy the information and have a look at what the doodlebuggers say is beneath the ground, the oil companies can decide if they want to make a bid to the government for the right to that particular oil lease.

Doodlebuggers do not always fill in the time between jobs by exploring on their own. Usually, if a new job is not available nearby, the doodlebuggers and their families and their equipment travel to one that is far away. The crew you will visit next is moving to the desert. It could be any of the world's great deserts—the Mojave in the United States, perhaps the Sahara of northern Africa, or the wilderness of the Sinai.

If the doodlebuggers are going to one of the deserts across the world, then the equipment is loaded onto freighters and shipped to the port closest to their new location. From the port, the equipment is driven into the desert. The doodlebuggers and their families fly to the area that will be their new home. As with the job on the North Slope, the doodlebuggers' families live in the closest town, while the doodlebuggers themselves go to the sandy dunes of the desert to live in tents while they shoot the line.

The party manager hires people from the town to be juggies

Soon the shifting desert sands will cover the tracks left by this doodlebugging parade.

for the crew. Although many, many doodlebuggers began their careers as juggies, most juggies do not travel great distances with the crew. The only juggies who stay with the crew and travel with it are the ones who are training to be shooters, or drillers, or surveyors, or perhaps even observers or party managers.

Doodlebuggers dress for the desert, just as they dress for the North Slope. Temperatures climb to over 130 degrees in the shade—when there is any shade! Doodlebuggers take a tip from the desert dwellers, who know how to handle its searing heat, and most of them keep their heads covered.

If the doodlebuggers are going to work on the Sinai, a special mine-clearing crew is called in. The area must be checked for land mines left over from the war between Egypt and Israel when the two countries fought for control of that area. If land mines are found, they are disarmed and removed before the doodlebuggers come in.

Both vibrating and shooting crews work in the desert, and once again it is up to the client to decide which type of crew he wants to use. But whether it is a shooting crew or a vibrator crew, the procedure for looking for oil is much the same the world over. It begins with the surveyor surveying the line. But sometimes surveying the line can get a little tricky—especially in the middle of the desert if the surveyor does not have a *bench mark.*

A bench mark is surveying talk for an established location. In other words, at a bench mark the latitude, longitude, and the elevation above sea level are known. Most countries put the correct bench mark on brass plates in many different locations as an aid to surveyors, because a surveyor must begin his calculations with a known starting point. But what if you

——————————No one wants to tussle with a tangled string of geophones, so at the end of a hot day's work in a Middle Eastern desert, this local juggie neatly puts the jugs away until tomorrow.

are in the middle of the Sahara, and you don't have a bench mark anywhere near? How can you begin to survey without a starting point? Well, if a surveyor has the right piece of equipment, he can get a satellite to tell him where he is.

Satellite navigation is a very sophisticated method of establishing your location when you have no idea where in the world you are, other than saying, "I'm in Tunisia in the middle of the Sahara desert." All you have to know is the date and the

approximate time of day, and—if you have a satellite navigation receiver—the satellite will do the rest of the work.

Some doodlebugging crews carry these receivers with them
to help the surveyors get started. It works like this. The United
States government has placed navigation satellites in orbit for
the specific purpose of helping people establish where they are
on the earth below. These satellites send out a signal that is
picked up by the satellite navigation receivers. The receiver
looks like a small box, as so many complicated instruments do.
There is an antenna that comes with the equipment, and the
antenna is set up on the ground a few feet from the receiver.
The antenna picks up signals from a satellite orbiting above.
The first information the satellite sends back may not be completely accurate; a lot depends on conditions in the atmosphere,
such as *static*, which is electrical interference, and the position
of the satellite's orbit. The computer does not like the satellite
to be orbiting near the horizon, but it doesn't want it to orbit
directly overhead either. In what doodlebuggers call a "good
pass", the orbit is somewhere in between those two positions.
The computer in the receiver knows when the satellite is making a good pass, and with each good pass the computer updates
and averages the information that it received from the previous
passes. Within twelve to twenty-four hours the satellite will
tell the surveyor the latitude, longitude, and elevation at that
particular spot in the world. He will know his latitude and
longitude within two to ten meters, and he will know how high
he is above sea level (his elevation) within one meter. A meter
is 3.28 feet. The surveyor will have his bench mark. It has
come to him from outer space, and it will help him and his
fellow doodlebuggers learn more about inner space—the area
buried beneath the earth's crust.

Once the line is surveyed, the juggies are ready to go to work setting out the cables in the scalding desert sands. If it is a shooting crew, the drill trucks roll across the sand and drill the holes for the explosives. The shot holes are loaded and the blaster is armed. In the doghouse, the observer decides the time is right for the shot, and he triggers it. Puffs of sand like low-lying clouds explode on the desert, and the earth trembles inside. The geophones listen to the trembling and send its sound back to the dog house, and the desert that was once an ocean begins to tell where its oil is hidden.

Like the vibrators, the drills the doodlebuggers use are sometimes mounted on buggies. These buggy-mounted drills bore the holes for the explosive charges.

_____The desert shakes when the shots go off, sending puffs of sand and smoke into the air.

At night, as the desert's temperature drops from very hot to very cold, the doodlebuggers return to their tents or trailers, just as the Bedouins who live there have done for centuries. The tent camp is set up in much the same way that the trailer camp was set up on the North Slope. However, up there the trailers were heated, but on the Sahara the tents are not air-conditioned!

A tent camp has sleeping tents, cooking tents, eating tents, and office tents. Like the trailer camps in the arctic, electricity for the tent camp is provided by a generator brought by truck to the desert site. Another thing the tent camp does not have is running water. The water, too, is brought to the camp by truck and stored in barrels. But even without running water, the doodlebuggers have a way to have a nice, warm outdoor shower at the end of a hard day in the desert.

To make their shower, the doodlebuggers take empty oil drums or other large barrels and paint them black. Black is a color that attracts heat from the sun and holds it. Next, they mount two or three of these containers on a stand that is about ten feet high. Then the doodlebuggers poke a hole in the side of the barrels, near the bottom, and insert a pipe. If they re-membered to bring them along, shower heads are screwed on to the end of the pipe. If they forgot them, then the water flows from the pipe as it does from your kitchen sink. A faucet to turn the water on and off is part of the shower, too. All day long, while the doodlebuggers work, the sun beats down on the black oil drums, and the water inside them begins to warm up. By the time the doodlebuggers return, warm showers are wait-ing for those who are first in line. As the sun goes down, the water in those drums cools off pretty quickly, and few doodle-buggers like a cold shower!

_____"Home Sweet Home" for doodlebuggers working in a desert in the Middle East is often a tent camp like this one.

A real danger for desert doodlebuggers is the possibility of getting lost. No one wanders away from the camp by himself—chances are he would not be able to find his way back. There are no landmarks in the desert; the world looks the same no matter what direction you look. The trail that your footprints make in the sand can be quickly covered up by the blowing and shifting sands. Doodlebuggers who must leave the tent camp and drive a truck across this sandy wasteland take a compass with them for guidance to the nearest town.

The doodlebuggers remain in the desert for several weeks at a time. At the end of that time, they take a break and return to the closest town to see their families and friends. When their break is over, they head for the sandy dunes of the desert once again. The world is thirsty for oil, and the doodlebuggers press on, shaking deserts that once were ocean bottoms to find it.

——————————Some things are the same all over the world. Even in the desert the laundry must get done.

Doodlebuggers have to learn to live under difficult conditions in many parts of the world, but perhaps some of the most difficult areas to work in are the world's jungles. The doodlebugger's search may take him into the jungles of Guatemala or the Philippines or Sumatra or Peru—anywhere there is a tropical forest that could be hiding oil.

Jungles are hot, steamy, sometimes beautiful, sometimes scary places. A jungle at high noon can seem as dark as evening if the tropical sun's light cannot penetrate its dense growth. Vines as thick as a man's thigh grow everywhere. Creeks and tributaries of rivers snake through the jungle's floor, and mud oozes everywhere. Parrots, monkeys, ocelots, snakes, tigers—all make their home here. They must wonder about this strange creature, the doodlebugger, as they peer out at him from their hiding places. Many times, no other human being has been where the doodlebugger is going.

But before the doodlebugger can begin to think about setting off his earthquakes in the jungle, the vines and undergrowth must be cleared away. If possible, bulldozers are taken to the jungle, and their blades scrape away a path for the trucks and equipment to drive in on. If the client has decided to use a vibrating crew, the vibrators are mounted on buggies so that they can twist in the middle as they make their way along the winding jungle path. Frequently, the many-ton vibrators sink into the muddy ooze on the jungle's floor, and there they remain until they are pulled out with cables and winches. It is a slow process, but the vibrators lumber on to the next spot on the line, and the trucks that might be needed to pull them out again tag along behind.

A parade of doodlebuggers must be a strange sight to this Guatemalan woman and her children.

_____It's easy to get stuck in the mud when you weigh thirteen tons. This vibrator may spend the night right here in the jungle.

Many times, the jungle is so dense and its floor is so irregular that it is impossible for bulldozers or trucks to enter. Then the path for the doodlebuggers must be cleared by hand. When the path is cleared by hand, local workers, using *machetes*, do the job. A machete is a kind of enormous butcher knife. It is useful for opening coconuts and chopping bunches of bananas from a banana tree. It can also be useful for saving someone's life.

Once, in the jungles of Trinidad, a local worker was using his machete to clear a path for a doodlebugging crew. Above him, in the branches of a banana tree, there was a slight movement that he did not notice. Suddenly, a boa constrictor dropped from the tree and wrapped itself around the chest of the man.

Boa constrictors kill their victims by suffocating them. Every time a boa's victim takes a breath, the deadly snake squeezes tighter. The victim can breathe out, but he cannot breathe in— without air he cannot call for help.

Another worker, who was also chopping underbrush, saw what had happened to his companion. Thinking quickly, he used his machete and hacked the boa constrictor to death.

Members of the doodlebugging crew rushed up when they saw what had happened. They removed the pieces of the boa constrictor and quickly got the man back to the crew's camp. At the camp, a helicopter was called, and the man was flown to a hospital in the closest town, where he was treated for a crushed chest and a broken arm—and a few machete cuts. Although the machete injured him, it also saved his life.

If machetes are used to clear a path for the doodlebuggers, then the crew is a *portable crew*. When a doodlebugging crew is portable, everything is carried to the line by hand.

—Men and machetes—a combination jungle doodlebuggers cannot do without.

Everything. Since it is obvious that no one can carry a vibrator,
you can easily see that all portable crews are shooting crews.

In order to move the instruments, local workers make *litters*
for them. A litter is a kind of stretcher, and these stretchers
are often made from bamboo that has been chopped down
with a machete. The instruments are lashed to the litters, and

the litters are lifted onto the shoulders of the men who will carry them down the jungle path to the location that will be the crew's new home.

Geophones and cables, survey instruments, tents—even the drills are carried in by hand. The new camp might be miles deep into the jungle, but distance does not bother the doodle-bugger—he goes where he thinks the treasure might be. The doodlebuggers either walk to their new home or, if there is a river running through the jungle, hollow out a log and paddle themselves there. Many of the rivers that snake through jungles where the doodlebuggers work are too narrow for a regular boat.

Once they are in the jungle and the tents have been set up, the doodlebuggers usually build a heliport. Native workers cut down trees and build this landing platform for helicopters. A helicopter is used to fly men and equipment and supplies back and forth from civilization to the jungle camp.

When the camp is established, the doodlebuggers are ready to go to work. Surveyors survey the line, and the drillers drill the holes for the charges, only this time they turn that drill stem by hand. The shot holes are loaded with explosives, and the geophones are attached to the seismograph. The shot goes off, the earth shakes, the geophones listen, and the seismo-graph records. Once again, the earth gives up its secrets.

As the crew shoots the line, it may have to travel far from the base camp. In that case, a *fly camp* will need to be set up. Fly camps are used when it is too far, or too difficult, at the end of a day's shooting to return to the base camp. A base camp, whether it has tents or trailers, can be rather comfort-able. A fly camp is very, very simple.

Local workers stay with the doodlebuggers who are using

Far from civilization a tent camp provides a base from which the doodlebuggers penetrate the thick jungle.

the fly camp. One of these workers is always a cook. Sometimes the cook has brought food from the base camp to prepare for dinner. Other times he and some other workers go hunting in the jungle for something to fix for dinner. If there is a stream running through the jungle, he might try to catch some fish— being very careful all the while to avoid catching any piranha.

Piranha fish are common in South America, where a lot of jungle exploration is done. Piranhas eat the flesh of men and animals. Many an unwary doodlebugger who thought a bath in a jungle stream sounded like a good idea has had fingers and toes sliced off by hungry piranha. When the natives of an area know of piranha in the water and they want to cross the stream, they slaughter an animal and throw the bleeding carcass into the river. The blood attracts the flesh-eating fish, who go after the carcass, leaving the humans free to cross.

After supper in the fly camp, when the doodlebuggers settle down to sleep, they either crawl into a hammock that has been carried in or climb up on a sleeping platform that has been built out of bamboo for them. The height of the sleeping platform discourages some jungle creatures from visiting the doodlebuggers while they are asleep. Fire also discourages animals from prowling around in the camp, so a fire burns all the time in a fly camp.

Mosquito nets cover the men when they sleep, even though the men have taken yellow fever shots before they leave home. They also take malaria pills each day to protect them from the mosquitoes carrying that disease, too.

But no matter how careful doodlebuggers are, there are times when they get sick. Sometimes they even die. Geophysical companies try to take care of everyone who works for them. If a local worker dies while he is working for a geophysical company, it is the company's responsibility to return him to his native village for burial.

In South America a few years ago, a young Peruvian Indian died while he was working for a geophysical crew. He did not have an accident; he simply became sick and died before anything could be done to help him. The Indian was deep in the jungle at a fly camp when it happened. The doodlebuggers managed to get his body back to the nearest town, but they could not find an airplane to fly the man to his village to be buried. The doodlebuggers had quite a problem. It was important that the man's body be buried quickly. The jungle is hot, and there are no funeral homes near there to embalm bodies. The only place available in the small town to store the body was the local icehouse, so the doodlebuggers wrapped the body in sheets and took it to the icehouse. They rented space from the owner while they continued to try to get an airplane. Fortunately, before the afternoon was over, a plane did come, and the man's body was removed from the icehouse and flown to his village. There the doodlebuggers and the village people gave the young native doodlebugger a proper burial.

In the jungles, and everywhere else they go, doodlebuggers must be prepared to deal with any emergency.

About 70 percent of the planet we call home is covered by water, and we earthlings live on the remaining dry 30 percent. You have been reading about the doodlebuggers who search for oil on that dry 30 percent, but there is treasure worth finding under the waters of the world, too.

Through *oceanography*, the study of the waters of the world and what goes on in them, we have learned that our oceans, rivers, lakes, and seas are all rich in many natural resources. Besides vast amounts of fish and plant life, there are deposits of copper, nickel, cobalt, manganese—even gold and silver—hidden in the ocean's depths. But even though we know these minerals are there, so far no one has found a way to recover them that would not cost more than the minerals themselves are worth.

However, there is one natural resource beneath the sea that we are able to retrieve. That resource is oil, and doodlebuggers take to the sea in seismic exploration boats to look for it.

No one owns an ocean. Governments own the mineral rights in the waters that border their countries, and they offer oil companies the opportunity to drill for oil in those waters. If an oil company obtains an oil lease in the waters of the North Sea or off the coast of Venezuela—or even New Jersey—it might hire a marine crew of doodlebuggers to shake the ocean's floor to find the best place to drill.

Once again, the doodlebuggers say good-by to their families. They look for oil in the waters of the Arctic and Antarctic circles, the Caribbean, the Dead Sea—anywhere the oil company wants them to go. When they leave their families, they will be gone for about a month. The seismic ships can stay at

——————————Looking like a giant spider, this seismic ship is
ready for a day's shooting. Air guns are lowered from rigid booms at
the side of the boat, and the hydrophone cables trail in the water
behind.

sea that long without returning to port for fuel and supplies.

There are really two crews involved in marine doodlebugging. There is the boat's crew, which consists of the captain, first mate, and other sailors whose major responsibility is the safe operation of the boat, and there is the doodlebugging crew itself, whose major responsibility is shaking the earth at the bottom of the ocean and listening for the returning echoes.

A marine crew has a party manager, just as a land crew does. The marine party manager usually does not go out to sea with the doodlebuggers. Instead, he remains on shore in constant radio contact with the ship. The party manager orders all the supplies the crew will need and communicates with the client. Out at sea, the person in charge of the doodlebuggers is the *coordinator*. The boat's captain and the coordinator work closely together. If the captain feels that the waters are too rough for the doodlebuggers to work safely, then he tells the coordinator, and the coordinator closes down the crew until the storm has passed. On the other hand, if the coordinator wants the crew to work on shifts twenty-four hours a day, then the captain sees to it that the boat continues to sail through the waters twenty-four hours a day, too.

Surveying a line out at sea is a little different than it is on land. Actually, on a boat the line is surveyed and shot at the same time, and a doodlebugger called a *navigator* is in charge of this operation. He relies on computers and radios to help him. Before the ship ever goes to sea, the doodlebuggers are told exactly where—the latitude and longitude—the line should start and end. The oil company also tells the doodlebuggers how far apart it wants the shots to be. This information—the starting and ending points of the line and the distance between the shots—is fed into a computer. The computer digests this information and comes up with a kind of map called a *preplot*. The preplot tells the navigator what the latitude and longitude should be for each shot. In other words, the preplot tells the navigator exactly where the boat should be when each shot goes off. But how does the navigator know if the boat is there or not? He relies on a base station back on land to help him.

Before the marine crew begins to work, surveyors establish two base stations on the coast in the general area where the doodlebugging boat will work. The surveyors know the exact location of these base stations because they have surveyed them from a bench mark. The base-station radios send out a coded signal that gives the latitude, longitude, and elevation of each station. On the boat, the navigator has an instrument that receives these signals and, from them, computes the latitude and longitude of the boat itself. The navigator looks at his preplot, which tells him where the boat *should* be when the shots go off, and he looks at his navigation instruments, which tell him where the boat actually *is*. The navigator constantly compares where the boat is with where it should be and guides the captain. A little faster, a little bit slower, two degrees port, one degree starboard—the captain and the navigator see to it that the boat is in the correct spot for each shot.

On some exploration boats, the navigator's work is automated, and all the captain has to do is look at a television screen which will tell him how far he is off the line, and which direction the boat is heading. He wants his indicator on the screen to read as near zero as possible, and he looks at the indicator and steers the boat accordingly. He checks his position against a satellite reading every time a satellite goes by.

Whether doodlebuggers are looking for oil on land or at sea, the principle is still the same. A loud sound is sent deep into the earth, and the echo of that sound is reflected back to the surface, where the seismograph measures its intensity and the length of time it takes it to return. Of course, it is a little bit different getting a sound, or shot, into the ocean than it is to get it into the dry earth. Obviously the doodlebuggers cannot use a vibrator when they are out at sea. In the past, they did explode dynamite in the water in order to make their sound, but the dynamite could not be exploded as far down in the ocean as the doodlebuggers would have liked. When the dynamite exploded too close to the water's surface, a huge column of water, called a plume, shot into the air. It took so much of the dynamite's energy to shoot this water into the air that there wasn't enough energy left to shake the ocean's floor the way it should be shaken.

Today, most marine crews use a device called an *air gun* to get the sound into the ocean. An air gun can fire at a depth of thirty-five to forty feet below the surface. At that depth, there isn't too much energy wasted on high plumes of water. The air gun works a little like the old jack-in-the-box toy you might have played with when you were much younger. Do you remember how much space Jack took up when he was out of his box? You squeezed him down into the box and carefully closed the lid. Then you turned a handle that played music, until the lid was triggered, and it opened. Jack sprang from the box with force. The air from an air gun works the same way.

To make an air gun, giant air compressors on board the ship squeeze air into a space that is 350 times smaller than the air would normally take up. This compressed, or squeezed, air is then forced down a high-pressure hose and into a tubular steel container, which is the air gun. Air guns are always used

_____Despite wind and water the work must go on, so doodlebuggers put on their slickers and reel out the hydrophones.

in groups of from at least ten to seventy or more, and the *gunner* is the doodlebugger responsible for compressing the air and loading the air guns. He sits in front of instruments that tell him what the pressure is inside his guns, and he can adjust the pressure if he needs to. He is also responsible for maintenance of the air guns on board the boat.

The air gun is lowered into the water at the exact depth the doodlebugger wants. Normally, the air gun "shoots" sixty-four times for every mile the boat travels down the line. The observer does not trigger the air gun in the same way that he triggers shakes and shots on land. Another computer on board the boat, a computer called a *synchronizer*, is used. The frequency of the shots is programmed into the synchronizer, which sets them off automatically. When the shots go off, the air guns shoot 4500 pounds per square inch of compressed air into the water, and the ocean's floor shakes.

The hydrophones that listen to the shake are lowered into the water from giant reels of cable on the back of the boat. These cables, which are two miles long, are towed behind the boat. The doodlebugging boat flies a flag that warns other ships in the area that something they cannot see is being towed. The cables have just the right amount of oil in them, so they just barely float. If the doodlebuggers want the cable to sink to a certain depth, they attach weights to them or use a heavier cable toward the front. The doodlebuggers control how deep a cable sinks by attaching a plastic winglike device to it. Because of its wings, this device is called a *bird*. The wings of the bird automatically adjust to hold the different parts of the cable at the same depth. For example, the water in the Persian Gulf is very salty, and the cables tend to float easily, so more weights are added and the wings of the bird adjust to keep the cable level. But the water of the Caribbean is not so salty, so when the doodlebugger sails there, he removes the weights to keep the cable closer to the surface. This cable control system keeps each section of the cable from going up or down more than one

——————————————The wings of the bird are adjusted to keep the hydrophone cable exactly where the doodlebuggers want it.

tenth the thickness of a human hair during the time it takes the hydrophones to hear the sound coming up from the ocean floor. Just as there are two or three days of experimental shooting and shaking before a land crew begins work, a marine crew takes a number of days to adjust the depth of the cables so that the hydrophones are in exactly the right place to do the best job.

Once the cables are at the depth the doodlebuggers want, the line is ready to be shot. The captain positions the boat at the beginning of the line. The navigator checks his instruments and then checks the location on his preplot—they should be the same. It is time to begin to shoot the underwater line. The seismograph is turned on, and so is the synchronizer. The captain begins to move the boat forward at the proper rate of speed so that it is in the right spot for each shot. The navigator helps him by telling him to speed up or slow down. The shots are going off automatically, so the doodlebuggers must adjust the boat's speed to them. In this case, no one has time to ask if the crew is ready for the next shot. The boat moves ahead, guided by the navigator. The hydrophones listen to each underwater explosion, which go off about every ten seconds, and send what they hear to the seismograph, which the observer is carefully watching in the doghouse on the boat.

Land crews usually work from sunup to sundown, but the crew on a doodlebugging boat works twenty-four hours a day. Each man takes a shift while other doodlebuggers rest or relax. The more modern boats have video-tape systems on board, so the crew can watch movies or taped television programs when they are not working. There is no point in having a regular television set on board, for the crew is too far from shore to pick up any television signals. Eating is always a popular pastime with doodlebuggers, and the ship's cook keeps the galley, or kitchen, well stocked with good things to eat.

Sometimes four-legged creatures, those who are invited and those who are not, join the doodlebuggers on board their seismic ships. One crew, working in the waters of the North Sea, took a cat named Trixie along with them. Trixie was a much-loved member of the crew who enjoyed stalking through the air-conditioning ducts of the boat. The strange sounds she made did not bother the doodlebuggers, who were used to her midnight prowls, but doodlebuggers who joined the crew after Trixie did were often spooked by the strange sounds coming from the ducts above their bunks.

On another doodlebugging ship, this one sailing in South American waters, another creature made an appearance. A doodlebugger was resting quietly in his bunk when he felt a tug on his sleeve. When he looked, he could see nothing, so he fell back asleep. In a little while, he was awakened again, and this time, he felt as if someone had nailed his arm to the wall. No one had nailed his arm to anything, but someone—or something—had pulled his sleeve through a tiny hole in the cabin wall, and his arm was still in the sleeve. The doodle-bugger twisted in his bunk so that he could peer through the hole in the wall. Peering back at him from the other side of the wall was a beady-eyed rat, who thought his sleeve would make some dandy padding for her nest. Trixie would have been a welcome addition to that boat's crew.

At the end of their time at sea, the doodlebuggers head back for port. The party manager collects the precious seismic rec-ords, and the doodlebuggers, landlubbers again, head for town to see their families and friends. The boat will stay in port for a little while to take on fresh supplies. Then, once again, it will head for the open sea, searching for treasure that lies far deeper than any booty on a sunken pirate ship.

CHAPTER

10

Meanwhile, back at the office . . . Not all of the doodlebugger's work is done out in the field. Huge numbers of people work in offices all over the world, doing jobs that make it possible for the shooting, shaking, and marine crews to do theirs.

Many geophysical companies build their own seismic instruments, so they employ electrical engineers to design them. Technicians must build these instruments carefully, according to the engineers' designs, so geophysical companies employ hundreds of electronic technicians to work at laboratory benches bringing the instruments to life and repairing them too.

Computers play an enormous role in the doodlebugging industry, and there is a great need for people capable of designing the complicated programs these computers use. A *program* is the instruction that tells a computer what to do, and as we have seen, doodlebuggers' computers must know how to do many different things. The computers that help the doodlebuggers do these jobs are the largest computers in the world, and they cost from six to eleven million dollars each. Many geophysical companies have several of these giant computers housed in data processing plants around the world.

When the seismic record comes from the seismograph out in the field, it has recorded all the sounds that the earth made as it was shot or shaken. But the earth is always shifting and moving a little, so it is always sending some kind of sound back to the surface. The geophones pick up all the sounds from the earth's surface—the ones the doodlebuggers cause and the ones that are made naturally. For example, when an air gun

—————————————All seismic instruments are made up of many delicate parts that often need repair. This woman solders carefully as she works.

explodes in the water, it makes a bubble in the ocean's depths. That bubble eventually bursts, and when it does, it makes a sound, too. The hydrophones pick up the sound of the bursting bubble along with the sounds from the trembling ocean's floor. The only sounds that the doodlebuggers are interested in—in fact, the only ones they want to hear—are the sounds caused by their shakes and shots. Doodlebuggers call any other sound that comes to the seismograph *noise*. Too much noise in a seismic record can distort that record and give the doodlebuggers and their client an inaccurate picture of the layers of

————Magnetic tapes from the doodlebuggers' seismographs wait their turn to be processed by giant computers that fill rooms like this one in geophysical data-processing plants around the world.

the earth. When the seismic records are put into a computer a special program takes the noise out of them, and only the right sounds remain.

When all the noise has been taken out of the seismic record, it is processed again by a computer, and the final result is a *seismic section.* If you know how to read it properly, a seismic section shows you exactly what the layers of earth below the prospect that was explored look like. In the geophysical industry, geophysicists and geologists read seismic sections and decide if the layers of earth contain oil traps. This process is called *interpretation.* Sometimes the client asks the doodlebugging company to interpret the section and sometimes the client does it himself. The interpreter looks at the seismic section, which shows him a cross section of the earth's layers as clearly as if some giant had taken a knife and sliced through it like a piece of layer cake. The interpreter then makes a set of maps from this seismic section, and they are truly treasure maps. The maps shows the shape of each of the layers of the earth that might be expected to have trapped some oil.

The doodlebugger's job ends with interpretation. He has made the treasure map, but only the client can decide whether to drill. Like any good treasure map, the doodlebugger's has an X that marks the spot, but no one can promise the client that if he digs, the treasure will be there. Only his drill can tell him if his search will be rewarded with black gold.

The doodlebuggers won't be there when the drills bite the dirt or plunge into the water. They will be off somewhere else, making seismic records, living in tents or trailers or boats, searching for oil in America, or Asia, or Africa, or Antarctica. As they search, they will find danger and excitement. Sometimes they will feel lonely and wish that they were home. But

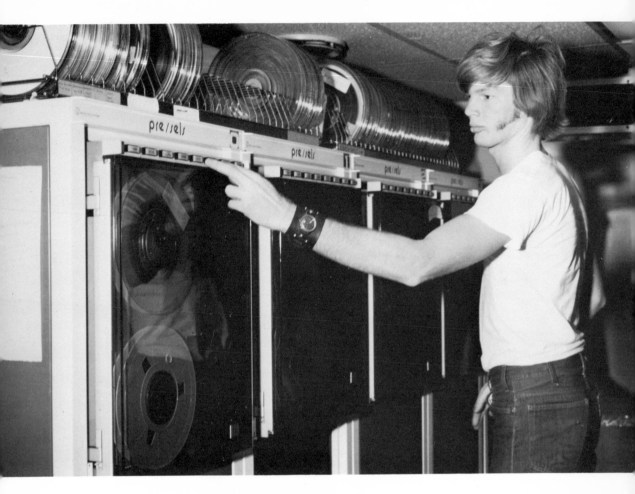

——————————Like a caterpillar that turns into a butterfly, this magnetic tape will change, too. It goes into the computer as a reel of tape, and is transformed into a seismic section—a true treasure map.

——————————————Any good treasure hunter studies his map carefully. These scientists are interpreting the seismic section to decide where— or if—**X** marks the spot where oil hides.

they keep on looking because, right now, the world simply has not found enough of that treasure.

Unlike the asphalt in Pitch Lake, it took nature an average of 250 million years to form the oil that we are finding today. We don't have time to wait for nature to make a fresh batch if we use it all up. We must use very carefully the oil that we do have, and we must continue to look for more.

You can help the doodlebuggers as they search for more energy for our world. How about remembering to turn out your light?

INDEX

earthquakes caused by, 21, 22, 26, 31, 34, 37, 43, 45
information sold by, 48
instruments used by, 17, 18, 20–21, 23, 25, 33
jungles explored by, 58, 61–66
marine, 22, 67–76, 79
and mechanics as crew members, 45
tent camps for, 55
town office space for, 35
trailers for, 40, 45, 46, 55
See also Geophysical exploration company
Drake, Edwin L., 12, 13, 15
Driller on crew, 31

Earthquake, 21, 22
caused by doodlebuggers, 21, 22, 26, 31, 34, 37, 43, 45
measured by seismograph: *see* Seismograph
Earth's crust, movement of, 5, 7
Earth's surface, buckling of, 7
Electricity, oil burned to generate, 14
Europe, and continental drift, 5
Eveleth, Jonathan, 12

Fairbanks (Alaska), 38, 46
Far East, shooting line in jungles of, 26

Fault, geological, 21
Florida, as oil-producing state, 27
Fly camp, 63, 66
Ford, Henry, 14

Galley on doodlebugging ship, 75
Gasoline, 12, 14
Geology, definition of, 16
Geophones (jugs), 23, 31, 33, 34, 35, 40, 45, 53, 77
Geophysical exploration company, 27, 29, 77
See also Doodlebuggers (geophysicists)
Geophysicists: *see* Doodlebuggers
"Good pass," and satellite navigation, 52
Gravimeter, 17, 18
Gravity, definition of, 18
Guatemala, 58
Gunner in marine doodlebugging, 72

Hydrophones, 23, 73, 74, 75, 79

Illinois, as oil-producing state, 13, 27
Indiana, as oil-producing state, 13
Indians, North American, 1, 10
Industrial Revolution, 10
Interpretation process, 80

Juggies, 23, 31, 33, 35, 40, 50,
    53
Jungles, explored by doodle-
    buggers, 58, 61–66
Junior observer on crew, 34

Kansas, as oil-producing state,
    13, 27
Kentucky, as oil-producing
    state, 13
Kerosene, 12, 13
Kier, Samuel, 12

Lease, oil: *see* Oil lease
Limestone, 9, 18
Line, shooting, 26
Litter for instruments, 62–63
Los Angeles (Cal.), 37
Louisiana, 37
    as oil-producing state, 27
Lubricating oil, 12

Machete, use of, 61
Magnetometer, 17, 18
Malaria pills, 65
Marine crew, 22, 67–76, 79
Mechanics on crew, 45
Meter, definition of, 52
Mineral rights, 27, 29, 67
Missouri, as oil-producing
    state, 27
Mojave Desert, 48
Montana, as oil-producing
    state, 27
Mosquito nets, use of, 65

Navigator in marine doodle-
    bugging, 69, 70, 75
Nebuchadnezzar, King, 1
Noise in seismic record, 80
    definition of, 79
North America, and continen-
    tal drift, 5
North Sea, 26, 67, 76
Nuclear power plant, 20, 21

Observer on crew, 34, 35, 45,
    53, 75
Oceanography, definition of,
    67
Ohio, as oil-producing state,
    13
Oil
    drilling for, 13, 27, 67, 80
    formation of, 3–5, 83
    lubricating, 12
    shale, 5
    uneven distribution of, 5
Oil company
    doodlebuggers hired by, 27
    information bought by, 48
    oil lease obtained by, 27, 29,
        67
Oil lease, 27, 29, 48, 67
    offered by U.S. government,
        47
Oil pool, underground, 7, 9
Oil shale, 5
Oil trap, 7–9, 23, 25, 80
Oklahoma, as oil-producing
    state, 27

Titusville (Pa.), Bissell's farm in, 12, 13
Trailers for doodlebuggers, 40, 45, 46, 55
Trinidad, 3, 61
Trixie (cat), 76
Truck, recording, 33, 34–35, 43
Tundra, 26, 38, 46

Underground oil pool, 7, 9

Venezuela, 67
Vibrator, 26, 37, 43, 45, 58

Vibrator crew, 22, 37, 43, 45, 50, 58
Vibrator point, 26
Video-tape system on seismic ship, 75

Water witch, 17
Wax for candles, 12
Whiteout, 46
Wildcatter, 14–15, 17
Wyoming, as oil-producing state, 27

Yellow fever shots, 65

622
SCO

Scott, Elaine

Doodlebugging

8095

DATE			